Curious Questions & Answers about... Prehistoric Animals

First published in 2021 by Miles Kelly Publishing Ltd
Harding's Barn, Bardfield End Green, Thaxted, Essex, CM6 3PX, UK
Unit 5A The Court, Ashbourne Industrial Estate, Ashbourne,
Co. Meath, A84 DP73, Eire

Copyright © Miles Kelly Publishing Ltd 2021

2 4 6 8 10 9 7 5 3 1

Publishing Director Belinda Gallagher
Creative Director Jo Cowan
Editorial Director Rosie Neave
Senior Editor Fran Bromage
Design Manager Joe Jones
Cover Designers Andrea Slane, Mark Penfound
Image Manager Liberty Newton
Production Jennifer Brunwin
Reprographics Stephan Davis
Assets Lorraine King

All rights reserved. No part of this publication may be reproduced, stored in a retrieval system, or transmitted by any means, electronic, mechanical, photocopying, recording or otherwise, without the prior permission of the copyright holder.

ISBN 978-1-83515-097-9

Printed in China

British Library Cataloguing-in-Publication Data
A catalogue record for this book is available from the British Library

Made with paper from a sustainable forest

www.mileskelly.net

Curious Questions & Answers about... Prehistoric Animals

"Who is your best friend?"

"Can you swim?"

"If you lived long ago would you prefer to be very small or very big?"

"What is your favourite food?"

"How many teeth have you got?"

Words by Camilla de la Bédoyère

Illustrations by Jack Viant

MILES KELLY

When did life begin?

The Earth was formed 4.5 billion years ago, but it took the first 4 billion years for animals to appear. They were small, slithering sea creatures, but over time, millions of other animals appeared.

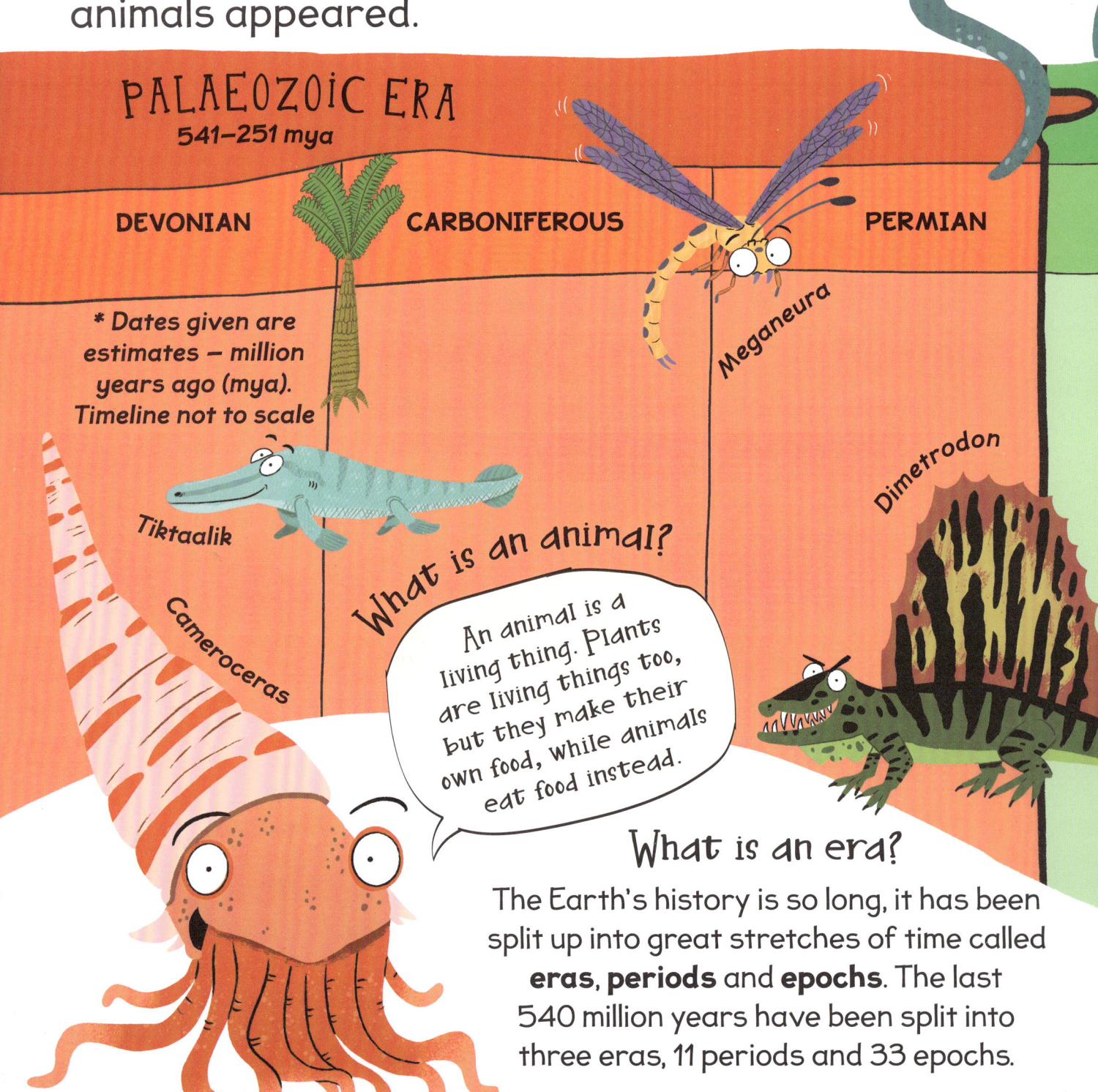

PALAEOZOIC ERA
541–251 mya

DEVONIAN — CARBONIFEROUS — PERMIAN

*Dates given are estimates – million years ago (mya). Timeline not to scale

Tiktaalik

Cameroceras

Meganeura

Dimetrodon

What is an animal?

An animal is a living thing. Plants are living things too, but they make their own food, while animals eat food instead.

What is an era?

The Earth's history is so long, it has been split up into great stretches of time called **eras**, **periods** and **epochs**. The last 540 million years have been split into three eras, 11 periods and 33 epochs.

Where are they all now?

If prehistoric animals ran out of food, or the planet got too hot or too cold for them, they died out and went extinct. Some prehistoric animals survived by slowly changing and adapting to new conditions. This is called evolution.

> Lots of animals, like dinosaurs, died out at the end of the Cretaceous Period when a massive meteorite hit the planet.

What is a fossil?

A fossil is the remains of a long-dead animal or plant that has been turned into stone.

① A dead animal is buried in mud, stones or sand

② Over a long time, hard body parts, such as shells, bones, teeth and claws are turned into stone

③ People dig up the fossils to study them

Which fish walked out of the sea?

Lobe-finned fish, like *Tiktaalik* did! They had strong leg-like fins, which they could use to swim or walk. *Tiktaalik* had lungs and gills, so it could breathe under water or in air.

We evolved to become tetrapods – the group of animals that live on land and walk on four legs.

Tiktaalik

We lived in the sea 400 mya and went extinct at the same time as the dinosaurs.

Ammonite

Dickinsonia

What's that blob of jelly?

Dickinsonia lived on the seabed, about 550 mya. It grew up to 80 centimetres long!

Did you know?

Pterosaurs were **NOT birds** – they were reptiles. Some of them lived at the same time as the first birds.

They had **leathery wings** that were attached to their hand bones and **freaky fourth fingers** that were extra long!

Pterosaur means **'lizard with wings'** and, like the dinosaurs, they all died out 66 mya.

The **largest** pterosaur was Quetzalcoatlus. It was the size of a **small plane**, and the largest animal ever known to fly.

Yikes!

The **smallest** pterosaurs were no bigger than a **sparrow**!

Was this mega-shrimp just a wimp?

Although Anomalocaris looked like a mighty killer, it probably only sucked up defenceless worms and jellyfish, rather than crushing big beasties. What do you think?

Anomalocaris

I was a metre long and had an armour-plated mouth.

Why are baby sea turtles super speedy?

They need speed to escape hungry hunters! Long ago, little ancient Archelons had to scuttle from the beach, where they hatched, into the sea before being eaten.

Archelon

I'll grow up to be the size of a small car.

Why were mammoths woolly?

Woolly mammoths lived during the Ice Age and grew thick fur to keep warm. When they died, their bodies often froze and were buried under thick layers of ice, which preserved them.

Woolly mammoth

Brrr!

Who got stuck in the mud?

Giant babies did! While Indricotherium mothers could wade through squelchy mud, their calves could get stuck and die, eventually turning into fossils.

Indricotherium

Mud was great for making footprints, which are called trace fossils

How many?

A fossilized Elasmosaurus was found with **197** pebbles in its tummy. The pebbles helped to grind up food.

A sabre-toothed fish's fangs were **6** centimetres long!

205,000,000 years ago was when the first furry animals evolved.

Andrewsarchus's skull was **1** metre in length — the biggest meat-eating mammal to ever live.

30 The number of hippos that weigh the same as one Sauroposeidon.

1.5 The weight in tonnes of the world's largest ammonite.

10 The number of tentacles of a *Cameroceras*. These squid-like creatures had a shell shaped like a giant ice-cream cone!

The longest dinosaur footprints ever discovered were **170** centimetres long (probably made by giant plant-eating dinosaurs called sauropods).

The length of a *Styxosaurus*'s neck was **6** metres – half of its entire body.

The oldest known fossil of a land-based animal is Kampecaris at **425** million years old.

0 The number of teeth *Shastasaurus* had. It probably sucked up and swallowed jellyfish whole.

Why were bugs so big?

Long ago there were mega-spiders, massive millipedes, and dragonflies the size of birds! They grew so big because the air contained more oxygen than it does today.

I was a giant plant-eating millipede.

Arthropleura

Scientists think Arthropleura could have grown to over 2 metres

Who had a sting in its tail?

Jaekelopterus was a giant scorpion — twice as big as you! Ancient scorpions preferred watery homes to hunt fish or frogs.

Jaekelopterus

Yikes!

I had nasty nipping pincers to grip my prey too!

Who snacked on dinosaurs?

Snap! My favourite meal is a tasty Ouranosaurus!

Sarcosuchus

— 120 pointy teeth

Massive predators often lurked in shallow, swampy water, waiting for thirsty dinos to come and drink. Sarcosuchus was the length of 10 of you!

Who needed just one meal a year?

I did! One big meal, like a crocodile, would last me a whole year! I was 13 metres long and I could get my jaws around almost anything.

Titanoboa

Titanoboa held its victim in its teeth and squeezed it to death before swallowing it whole.

What were those claws for?

Although Therizinosaurus had terrifyingly sharp, metre-long curved claws, they were probably only used to strip leaves from trees. They might also have been used to defend itself.

Don't panic — I'm a vegetarian! I'm as big as a T rex, but not as mean.

Therizinosaurus

Did ancient animals need friends?

Hunting together meant that predators like Hyaenodon could catch and kill animals bigger than themselves, like Daeodon.

Our jaws were strong enough to crush bone!

Daeodon

Hyaenodon

Would you rather?

Be as **snappy** as Xiphactinus or as **prickly** as a prehistoric worm?

Knit a **scarf** for a Diplodocus or take a T rex to the **dentist**?

Hide inside a Glyptodont's shell or try your luck in a **cave** with Arctodus?

Eat **veggies** all day like Megacerops, or dine on dinosaur **eggs** like an ancient snake?

Could dinosaurs fly?

Many dinosaurs had feathers to keep them warm. Some small, feathered dinosaurs eventually began to fly and evolved to become the first birds, like Archaeopteryx.

Archaeopteryx lived about 150 million years ago.

Elephant bird

Archaeopteryx

"We had tiny wings and couldn't fly."

Which bird laid the biggest egg?

The largest bird eggs were laid by elephant birds. One egg would have weighed as much as 150 chicken eggs.

Elephant bird egg

Chicken egg

Confuciusornis: I could only fly short distances between trees.

Moa: We could grow to over 3 metres tall.

Phorusrhacos

Which bird was a giant?

Many prehistoric birds grew big, but moas were the tallest birds ever known. They lived in New Zealand and were hunted by humans. They probably went extinct 500 years ago.

This terror bird couldn't fly, but it was fast on its feet

Did early birds catch worms?

Yes – early birds ate worms, bugs, fish and seeds. Some big birds, known as terror birds, were deadly hunters of larger animals.

Which gentle giant had a bad temper?

Megatherium was a sloth as huge as an elephant. It could stand up on its back feet and use its dagger-like claws to slash at attackers.

I may look like a sleepy sloth, but if you scare me I'll turn nasty!

Megatherium

What's the point in awesome antlers?

Male deer today use their antlers to fight each other at mating time. *Megaloceros* was an ancient deer that did the same thing, with awesome antlers 3 metres across!

Each tip of a deer's antlers is called a point

Antlers are made of bone.

Megaloceros

What is an ancestor?

An ancestor is an early type of animal that has modern relatives. *Eosimias* was an early type of tiny monkey that lived about 40 mya. Ten million years later, a larger monkey had evolved.

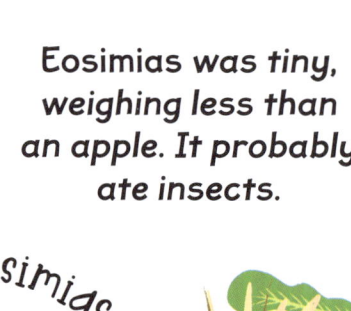

Eosimias was tiny, weighing less than an apple. It probably ate insects.

Eosimias may have been an ancestor of all modern monkeys and apes.

Could a bird eat a horse?

Yes! Some early horses were as small as a pet cat. They made a tasty snack for giant birds.

Tiny *Propalaeotherium* could hide from predators in dense, shady forests.

Sifrhippus was about the size of a small dog.

A compendium of questions

Why all the strange names?

When scientists find a new animal they can name it after themselves or where it was found, use Latin or Greek, or make up a new name.

I'm going to call you... Dave.

Who has cube-shaped poo?

Today's wombats make little cubed poos, but fossilized poo found from giant wombats is round.

Which frog could bite like a cat?

Beelzebufo was a prehistoric frog with a sticky tongue and a deadly bite. It could even kill baby dinosaurs!

Yikes!

What was the biggest fish?

Leedsichthys is a contender for the award of largest fish to ever live – reaching at least 16.5 metres long.

Which cat was a copycat?

Miracinonyx! It looked like a cheetah, but was probably a type of mountain lion. It could run at 70 kilometres an hour!

Have camels always had humps?

No. Synthetoceras had a flat back, but two horns on top of its head and a Y-shaped horn on its nose!

How did insects end up in amber?

Insects were often trapped in the sticky sap from trees. Once dry the sap became orange stone, called amber, with the bugs preserved inside.

When did prehistory end?

Humans began writing history around 5400 years ago — marking the end of prehistory and the beginning of history!

What was the largest mammal to ever live on land?

Indricotherium was about 5 metres tall, but could stretch far higher with its long neck.